Mysteries
OF LOST
CIVILISATIONS

PUFFIN BOOKS

Published by the Penguin Group
Penguin Books Ltd, 27 Wrights Lane, London W8 5TZ, England
Penguin Putnam Inc., 375 Hudson Street, New York, New York 10014, USA
Penguin Books Australia Ltd, Ringwood, Victoria, Australia
Penguin Books Canada Ltd, 10 Alcorn Avenue, Toronto, Ontario, Canada M4V 3B2
Penguin Books (NZ) Ltd, 182–190 Wairau Road, Auckland 10, New Zealand

Penguin Books Ltd, Registered Offices: Harmondsworth, Middlesex, England

First published by Aladdin Books/Watts Books 1996
Published in Puffin Books 1998
1 3 5 7 9 10 8 6 4 2

Copyright © Aladdin Books Ltd, 1996
All rights reserved

Designed and produced by Aladdin Books Ltd, 28 Percy Street, London W1P 0LD

The author, Dr Anne Millard, has a Ph.D. in Egyptology from University College, London. She
is the author of numerous books on ancient Egypt and other aspects of the ancient world. She
has excavated in Egypt and lectures for the Extra-Mural Department of the University of
London.

The consultant, George Hart, is an Egyptologist working at the Education Section of the British
Museum, London. He has written extensively on ancient Egyptian books and pyramids.

Editor: Katie Roden
Design: David West, Children's Book Design
Designers: Edward Simkins, Flick Killerby
Picture Research: Brooks Krikler Research
Illustrators: Francis Phillipps; Stephen Sweet – Simon Girling and Associates; Rob Shone

Made and printed in Belgium

British Library Cataloguing in Publication Data
A CIP catalogue record for this book is available from the British Library

ISBN 0–141–30067–1

Mysteries
OF LOST
CIVILISATIONS

ANNE MILLARD

PUFFIN BOOKS

6. Cadbury Fort
7. Stonehenge
8. Corsica
9. Carthage
10. Alexandria
11. Amarna
12. Abu Simbel
13. Meroe
14. Nubia
15. Great
    Zimbabwe
16. Crète
17. Thera
18. Olympia
19. Mycenae
20. Anatolia
21. Troy
22. Palmyra
23. Qumran

1. Rock Eagle Mound
2. Tenochtitlan
3. Lake Guatavita
4. Nazca Lines
5. Machu Picchu

24. Babylon
25. Edom
26. Dilmun
27. Bactria
28. Indus Valley
29. Altai tombs
30. Amazonian graves
31. Mount Li
32. Angkor
33. Easter Island

CONTENTS

"...a search in which whatever was not removed was deliberately and avowedly destroyed in order to enhance the intended profits of European speculators."

Archaeologist Sir W.M. Flinders Petrie, condemning the treasure hunters at Abydos, Egypt, 1901-2

Introduction to THE MYSTERIES

Unravelling the mysteries of the past is not easy. Many ancient peoples did not use writing, so their ideas and deeds are forgotten. Written evidence can tell us what people believed, what they did, what they thought and what others thought of them. But it is important to be careful when reading texts. If the only surviving record of a civilisation is written by its enemies, will it be a fair account?

Time is the eternal enemy of archaeologists (people who study the past) – only a few bodies and objects survive decay. Many other things can destroy clues to the past, such as natural disasters, wars, religious upheavals, farming, building – and even careless servants! They often survive only by chance. So, for an accurate view of the past, archaeologists have to turn detective, examining buildings and objects, studying texts and listening to what legends can tell them. They also need the help of all the latest scientific techniques.

Hidden PLACES

Some places are destroyed and disappear, almost without trace, until an archaeologist tracks down their remains. Sometimes a place is mentioned only in a much later text and is dismissed as a legend.

A good example is the siege of Troy (in modern-day Turkey) by the ancient Greeks. For centuries, the *Iliad* (700s BC), Homer's poem about the Trojan war, was regarded as fantasy. But an amateur archaeologist called Heinrich Schliemann passionately believed that it was true. In 1870, he began digging in the area where Homer had placed Troy – and found it! Excavations have proved that Homer knew a great deal about a civilisation that had vanished centuries before he was born. Stories and songs had kept alive memories of such details as the city's defences and the soldiers' armour. We cannot yet prove that the beautiful Helen of Troy existed, or what the wooden horse was (left), but we have learnt not to simply dismiss the legends of the past.

*"Was this the face that launch'd a thousand ships
And burnt the topless towers of Ilium?"*
Description of Helen of Troy in Christopher Marlowe's play *Doctor Faustus*, c. 1588

L o s t   a n d FOUND

Many buildings referred to in ancient writings are now totally destroyed, such as the Roman emperor Nero's fabulous Golden House. Sometimes we find ruins that can be identified beyond doubt, like Pompeii in Italy, which was buried by a volcanic eruption. But even if archaeologists can identify a site and have ancient texts describing it, they still have difficulty imagining what it was like at its peak. Ancient Greek writers said that the burial complex of King Amenemhat III of Egypt was one of the most magnificent buildings they had ever seen; now, only dreary piles of mud bricks are left! Only if we have a picture of such a place can we begin to imagine it in all its glory.

Can destruction ever have benefits? Sometimes it can reveal other treasures. During the Second World War, a bomb destroyed the ancient church of St Bride's in London. This tragedy gave archaeologists a chance to excavate the site. They found earlier churches going back about 1,400 years and a Roman pavement from the second century AD. St Bride's was then rebuilt.

ROUND TABLE RIDDLES
In medieval legend, Camelot was the headquarters of King Arthur. If it existed, it was nothing like the fairy-tale castles of Hollywood films! It may have been an old Celtic hill-fort, reoccupied by the British war-leader – a place of earth ramparts and wooden battlements. Archaeologists have found such a site at Cadbury Fort in England, which some people think might be Camelot.

GARDENS OF LEGEND
The Hanging Gardens of Babylon were built for a queen from the hill country, who was homesick on the plains of Babylonia. They were so thoroughly destroyed that we cannot even identify the foundations for sure. There are many theories as to what they looked like!

ON THE TRAIL OF KING MINOS
In 1893, the archaeologist Arthur Evans was shown some seal-stones covered with strange images. He tracked them to Crete, the legendary home of King Minos. Evans began to dig, and unearthed the mighty Minoan civilisation. It had been ruined and forgotten – except in legend.

THE LIGHT OF THE MEDITERRANEAN
Built in about 280 BC, the lighthouse of Alexandria, in Egypt, was 117 m (390 ft) high. Its beam of light could be seen for 50 km (30 miles). It was toppled by an earthquake in the 1300s, but we still have accounts and pictures of it. Pieces of it have been found in the harbour.

An Indian mystery
Excavations by Sir Mortimer Wheeler (1890-1976) revealed artefacts (below), seal-stones (left) and buildings of the ancient Indus Valley civilisation in India. They had invented their own writing system, but no one has managed to decipher it yet. Will we ever know who their rulers were, the purpose of their great ceremonial bath or the identity of their god, the Lord of the Animals?

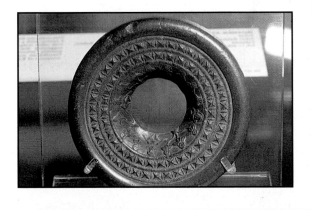

A GREAT TRIBUTE
In the fifth century BC, the Greek sculptor Pheidias made a vast statue of the god Zeus to go in the temple at Olympia. It was 13 m (43 ft) tall and made of gold and ivory. In AD 393, a Roman emperor took it to Constantinople, but a fire swept the place where it was kept in AD 462, destroying it completely.

THE EFFECTS OF WAR
Conquerors often try to wipe out all traces of their enemies' culture. This was the fate of the Aztec and Inca peoples at the hands of sixteenth-century Spanish explorers. The great Aztec capital of Tenochtitlan was demolished. Its remains still lie under modern Mexico City.

The Stuff of LEGENDS

When something really exciting happens, people like to tell the story over and over again. Unless it is written down immediately, it changes as time passes. Details get left out; others are added; the deeds of two or more people can be credited to one 'super-hero'. Over time, people even forget what some things were or what they meant, so they invent explanations – which are often wrong! A story might be given a new meaning so that it fits in with the politics and religion of the time. But somewhere, buried in every story, there remains a kernel of truth.

CONQUISTADORES!
The early Spanish conquerors of America were driven by a desire to serve God (by converting people to Christianity) and their king (by winning him an empire). But they were also ruthless and greedy, out to make their own fortunes from the gold and silver of the 'New World'. In Colombia, they heard the fantastic but true story of El Dorado – the 'Gilded Man' (see page 13).

Lake Guatavita (Colombia)

SOUTH AMERICA

THE ULTIMATE QUEST
People have searched all over the world for Atlantis (see page 13), but many now believe that the story was inspired by Minoan Crete (see page 11). The memory of the great island with its powerful navy, the importance of bulls in its religion and its sudden decline had become mixed up with natural disasters and myths. The stories were muddled and misunderstood as time passed, but some accounts do seem to contain an echo of the great Minoan civilisation.

THE GOLDEN RULER

When a king came to the throne in the region of Lake Guatavita, Colombia, he was covered in gold dust then sailed to the middle of the lake, where he threw in gold offerings to the gods. Imagination and greed embroidered the story, and tales spread of a city and a land made of gold. For two centuries, people searched for 'El Dorado' and it cost many lives. Others tried to drain the lake, but failed.

ERUPTION AND DEVASTATION

Thera (now Santorini), 120 km (72 miles) north of Crete, was an outpost of Minoan culture. In about 1450 BC, there was a huge volcanic eruption which destroyed most of the island. It also caused a tidal wave that wrecked Minoan settlements in northern Crete.

THE STUFF OF LEGENDS

The Greek writer Plato (above) wrote about Atlantis, a lost island kingdom which sank below the waves in a terrible disaster. Debates have raged ever since. Did Plato invent it? Was it based on Thera and Crete? Or was it another lost place? The tale had been passed on by word of mouth for almost 200 years before Plato heard it – plenty of time for errors to creep in!

Thera (Santorini)

King Solomon's mines

Some people have embarked on quests for things mentioned in the Bible – the Ark of the Covenant, the treasures from the temple of Jerusalem, Noah's Ark and many others. Others have looked for places. The fabulous mines of King Solomon caught people's imagination and inspired films and novels. When the ruins of Great Zimbabwe (below) were found in Africa, some suggested that these were the famous mines. But Zimbabwe belongs to a much later African empire. Solomon's mines remain out of our grasp.

Can texts really lead us to lost places? Ancient Mesopotamian texts refer to a place called Dilmun, describing it as so wonderful that, until recently, scholars dismissed it as fantasy. Studies of earlier texts and ruins have shown that it was a staging post in the trade between Sumer and the Indus Valley. When the trade ceased, Dilmun was forgotten – in fact, it was the island of modern-day Bahrain!

The Lost CULTURES

All cultures change over time. We can follow the developments of long-lived civilisations, like those of ancient Egypt and China, over thousands of years. We can see how life has evolved in Europe since the fall of the Roman Empire in AD 476. People's ways of life have changed, but we can trace elements from the past to the present.

Even if a culture seems to have been wiped out, some things survive and are absorbed by a new civilisation. Memories of lost cultures may live on in texts or in legends. Then one day, archaeologists may find solid remains. Archaeologists often discover many surprises while exploring lost cultures. Some people still find it hard to accept that young Minoans (left) would leap through the horns of charging bulls – yet there are pictures and statues to prove it. Did they risk their lives in this way to please a god? Perhaps they believed that this god tossed their land with earthquakes as the bull tossed the athletes with its horns.

"...[the archaeologist] brings to light a mass of objects illustrating the arts and handicrafts of the past, the temples in which men worshipped, the houses in which they lived, the setting in which their lives were spent."

Sir Leonard Woolley, *Digging up the Past*, 1940

Decline, Destruction
AND DEATH

Some flourishing cultures have been quickly and totally destroyed, but this rarely happens so dramatically. Usually, many factors combine and there is a long, slow decline to extinction. Years of bad weather may cause famine, farmland can lose its fertility if over-used, and wood supplies run out if people cut down trees without replanting them. A vital river may change course or a harbour may silt up. Earthquakes, floods and other natural disasters may occur. Trade may be disrupted or there may be wars and invasions. The people of a declining society may simply emigrate or decide to adopt the ways of more successful neighbours.

How do cultures become legends? Through distortions of fact that happen over time. For example, one group of the Sea Peoples (see page 17) was called the Peleset. After their defeat by Egypt, they retreated and the land where they settled was named after them – Palestine. They appear in the Bible as the Philistines, the arch-enemies of the Hebrews.

(see page 17)

OMENS OF DISASTER
A fiery comet in the early 1500s terrified the Aztecs of Central America. Was this a sign that their gods were angry with them? For ten years, many odd events occurred. The Aztecs thought they were doomed; and they were – the Spaniards arrived (see page 12).

(see page 12)

THE INCAS' LAST STAND
In 1911, the explorer Hiram Bingham set out for the Andes, armed with texts telling of cities where the last Incas had fought off the Spaniards. He found Machu Picchu, an Inca city that for 300 years had been hidden by the jungle.

THE MYSTERIOUS MYCENAEANS
After the decline of the Minoans, the Mycenaeans dominated trade in the Mediterranean Sea. They were rich and successful, but they declined too. By 1000 BC, their civilisation, artefacts (above) and writing system (right) had vanished. Only in legend did they and their heroes, such as Agamemnon, survive.

MYTHS OF THE MAYA

The Maya were once seen as a peace-loving people. But archaeologists have begun to decode their writing and it is clear that rival city-states fought constantly for power. Over-farming contributed to their decline, but so did these wars.

An advanced culture

The state of Meroe flourished from about 550 BC to AD 350 and traded with Egypt, Africa, Greece, Rome and India. Its culture was a blend of local ways and those of Egypt and other countries (such as pyramid tombs for its kings, below). Meroe's farmers grew cotton, imported from India. Its metal-smiths worked iron and their methods spread into Africa. One text claims Meroe was so rich that its prisoners were held in golden chains! Attacks by other peoples led to its decline, but it collapsed after an invasion by the King of Axum in East Africa.

River Nile

EGYPT

•Meroe

NUBIA

ATEN'S CITY

One king of Egypt, Akhenaten, believed that Aten was the only god. He built a new capital at Tel el Amarna and banned worship of other gods. But after his death, Amarna was left to the mercy of the desert sands.

INVADERS FROM THE SEA

Ancient Egyptian texts describe invasions by mysterious 'Sea Peoples'. These were from the declining Mycenaean empire, looking for new homes. In about 1190 BC, they invaded what is now Turkey, wiping out the Hittites (see page 18). They were finally defeated by Ramesses III of Egypt, and scattered all over the Mediterranean.

Who Were THEY?

THE KEY TO A LOST PEOPLE
In the 1970s, strange items (left) appeared on the antiques market. Scholars investigated them and tracked down a whole new culture, which had flourished in Bactria in 2500-1500 BC. The Bactrians were wealthy traders who controlled the land route between the Indus Valley and Mesopotamia.

As well as buildings and artefacts, one clue to a people's identity is its language. One very ancient language was Proto-Indo-European. Over the centuries, the groups who spoke it drifted apart. They travelled across Europe and into the Middle East, then to India and Turkestan. Each group changed its language so much that they would not have been able to communicate if they had met. This family of languages, now called Indo-European, includes almost all European languages, Russian, Ukranian, Armenian, Iranian and most of the languages of India and Pakistan, as well as many ancient languages.

HITTITE CONQUESTS
By 2000 BC, the Hittites had arrived in Anatolia from north of the Black Sea. They gradually established an empire and a writing system (below). At first they were Egypt's enemies, but then they sealed a treaty. They were wiped out by the Sea Peoples (see page 17).

Brutal invaders... or peaceful settlers?
Because it was their victims who wrote the records of their actions, the Vikings have been regarded as pirates for centuries. Some were, but most were farmers and skilled craftspeople. Others were daring merchants who travelled as far as the Middle East. There were also intrepid explorers who founded colonies in Russia, Iceland, Greenland and North America.

THE FIRST MINOANS

In about 6000 BC, the ancestors of the Minoans arrived on the island of Crete, probably from Anatolia. Archaeologists have traced their progress from simple farmers to a great trading nation. They invented their own writing system, which we call Linear A, but as yet no one can read it. Linear B, the writing of the later Mycenaeans (see page 16), is readable because it was an early form of Greek, which is an Indo-European language.

THE ROSE-RED CITY

In the fourth century BC, an Arab tribe, the Nabataeans, set up a kingdom in what had been Edom. They controlled the trade routes from Arabia and the Red Sea to the Mediterranean, and so became rich and powerful. Their great capital, Petra, was built of a pinkish stone and surrounded by cliffs. Its entrance was a narrow cleft in the rocks, while its temples and tombs were cut into the cliffs. It came under Roman rule in AD 106, and gradually declined.

THE MISSING MARVELS OF ANGKOR

The Khmers of Cambodia expanded their empire after AD 800 and built a great temple complex at Angkor Wat and a capital at Angkor Thom. But the Thais defeated them in the early 1400s and their buildings were lost in the jungle. They were found by chance, by Henri Mouhot in 1860.

What is the oldest alphabet?
The Phoenicians had invented a simple writing system by 1300 BC. It was the first alphabet. Three hundred years after the disappearance of Mycenaean Linear B, this system was adapted by the ancient Greeks to form their alphabet.
The only letter they did not alter was O – the world's most ancient written letter.

"*Moreover, all this ruin was brought upon the Romans by a woman, a fact which in itself caused them the greatest shame.*"

Dio Cassius of Rome, writing over 100 years after Boudicca's revolt

Missing PEOPLE

A society may record the deeds of its great men and women but, over time, the texts can be lost or destroyed. Our knowledge about them is therefore limited, but there is always hope that an excavation will find more texts!

If the few accounts of an event are written by one side only, they are likely to be biased. The British revolt of AD 60-61, led by Queen Boudicca of the Iceni tribe, is a good example. It killed thousands of Roman colonists and soldiers, important towns were destroyed and Rome nearly lost its new land. But the Romans won in the end and wrote of a struggle of law, order and civilisation against savagery and ignorance. Boudicca and the Britons who died were portrayed as fierce barbarians. If the Iceni had kept records, they might have described their heroic struggle to drive out invaders whose greed, cruelty and brutal treatment of Queen Boudicca had made them unworthy of being treated with honour or mercy.

The Forgotten
WOMEN

Our knowledge about women in history is limited. This is partly due to destruction of records over time, and partly because some societies were ruled by men who believed women were of little importance and so denied them any rights or power outside the home. The records of such a culture give few details about women. If a male-dominated society was threatened by a woman, its writers usually did their best to blacken her name. We can find many 'lost' women through texts and excavations, but we must be very careful not to be fooled by the attitudes of the authors of the texts!

How did Queen Boudicca die?
After her defeat, in AD 62, Boudicca committed suicide rather than be taken prisoner by the Romans. Records say that the Iceni gave her a costly burial, but it is not clear where. Several places in Britain claim the honour of being the site of the queen's last resting place. One theory says that she lies under Platform 8 of London's King's Cross railway station! Will this mystery ever be solved?

A KING WITH A DIFFERENCE
Women were honoured in ancient Egypt but only a man could ascend to the throne. A few women got round this rule. Queen Hatshepsut claimed that the god Amun had chosen her to rule and reigned as 'King'. After her death, her nephew destroyed her monuments to remove all traces of her. Archaeologists are now defeating him by putting the pieces back together again!

PAYING THE PRICE
Zenobia, Queen of Palmyra in Syria, carved her own empire by conquering Rome's eastern provinces. When she was finally defeated, the

Romans tried to humiliate her by making her walk in the emperor's victory parade – but she had the last laugh. She married a senator and became a famous hostess!

THE MYSTERIOUS QUEEN

Nefertiti was the wife of Akhenaten (see page 17). After their deaths, their enemies tried to destroy all records of their religious revolution, leaving us with many questions. Did Nefertiti support her husband's worship of Aten? Did she become 'King' for a while? When and how did she die?

THE MOST FAMOUS QUEEN IN HISTORY

Our information about Queen Cleopatra VII comes mainly from Roman records. She had scared the Romans by marrying Mark Antony and helping him to struggle against Octavian (later Emperor Augustus). She was a good ruler, but the Roman writers described her as unworthy.

THE LEGEND OF SHEBA

The Bible tells how the Queen of Sheba learnt of the wisdom of King Solomon and went to visit him. In fact, Sheba's kingdom was rich from trade. She and Solomon were probably making a trade deal!

BURIED IN STATE

Wonderfully preserved in an intricate tomb, surrounded by treasures and wrapped in beautiful silks, a mysterious Chinese noblewoman was discovered by archaeologists in the 1980s. Modern medical techniques have revealed the illnesses she suffered from and how she passed her final hours.

A scandal in Rome

Legend says that a young woman once disguised herself as a man and was elected Pope (the head of the Catholic Church)! She was nicknamed 'Pope Joan'. The story may have arisen because in the tenth century AD there were some very weak Popes. A mother and daughter called Theodora and Marozia gained influence over several of them, even deciding who the new Popes should be!

People of LEGEND

Every country and culture has its legends. It is tempting to quote a legend to help prove a theory about a piece of history, but we must use legends with great care. A legend may be based on real events but it is not always clear which bits are true; which are based on fact but have been changed; and which are later additions. It can be exciting if, while studying a text or excavating a site, archaeologists find something that fits in with or explains a legend; but they do not normally set out to prove that a legend is true.

THE BEAST IN THE LABYRINTH
Legend says the Minotaur was half bull, half man. He lived in the Labyrinth (maze) at Knossos, Crete, and ate human flesh. How did the story begin? Did later people misinterpret tales of bull-leaping? Perhaps Minoan kings wore bull masks for religious rites and this custom inspired the legend.

The eternal king
Charlemagne (AD 742-814), ruler of the Franks, in modern-day France and Germany, was an amazing man – a military leader, conqueror and supporter of the arts. Memories of him dominated Europe for years after his death. Minstrels soon began to exaggerate his achievements to make him seem even greater. So the Gascons he fought became Saracens, because at the time the Saracens were Europe's greatest enemy. It was even said that he was not dead but would return to rule one day.

RIDING THROUGH THE GLEN

England's best-loved folk hero is Robin Hood... but who was he? Over the centuries, writers and poets have altered his identity to suit the views of the time – from a peasant to an earl!

Was Robin Hood one man, or did the deeds of several outlaws get credited to one person? Legend places Robin in the reign of King Richard I (1189-99), but an outlaw called Robin Hood is recorded as living later. Did he use the name of the earlier outlaw, or was he the real one?

A TERRIBLE SACRIFICE

When civil war raged in eighteenth-century West Africa, legend says that Queen Pokou and her people fled for safety, but their journey was halted when they reached a vast, swiftly flowing river. In return for a safe crossing, the gods demanded the sacrifice of a child. Pokou could have killed a poor woman's child, but she sacrificed her own son.

Do legend and reality ever get mixed up? Myth and fact often become confused as a story is passed down through the centuries. For example, legend says that an early Count of Anjou, in France, met a beautiful girl called Melusine in a wood. He fell in love, married her and they lived happily – until he found out that she was the daughter of the Devil! Melusine's descendants are said to include England's Plantagenet kings (1154-1399), the ancestors of Britain's present royal family.

WARRIOR WOMEN

Greek writers told how Mycenaean heroes fought the Amazons, a tribe of women, who settled in what is now Russia. Scholars dismissed the stories, but in the 1950s archaeologists found the graves of a nomadic tribe in Russia. Some women's graves contained weapons and armour of the right date for the Amazons.

ROUND TABLE RIDDLES

Who was the real King Arthur? Early texts suggest he was a Roman Briton who fought the Saxons. Details like the sword Excalibur, his knights and the Round Table came later. When the Saxons won, some Britons fled to Wales, where bards reworked the story. Medieval minstrels, fifteenth-century poets and Victorian writers added to it, creating the legend as it is today.

> *"Whether you like it or not,
> history is on our side.
> We will bury you!"*
>
> Nikita Khrushchev, President of
> the former USSR, in a speech to
> Western ambassadors, 1956

Mysterious OBJECTS

Considering the destruction caused by time, nature and people, an amazing number of buildings, texts and objects have survived! But these represent only a tiny fraction of the glories of past civilisations. A site can be destroyed and completely lost if we have no references to it in any texts.

Texts mention many places, but we do not know where they were. Some are found by careful investigation. Sometimes we know where a city was but it is difficult to get at – the ruins of Pompeii, for example. The Romans destroyed the city of Carthage, in North Africa, but, thanks to careful excavation, archaeologists are finding out about Rome's great rival and know what its magnificent harbour and splendid docks were like (left).

Some people just cannot resist a challenge! They continue to search for objects and places that most scholars believe no longer exist, such as biblical objects like Noah's Ark and the Ark of the Covenant.

The Lost
BOOKS

It is bad enough when books and the vital information they hold are destroyed by accident. It is awful if they are tampered with to fit the ideas of the day. But history is littered with instances of the deliberate destruction of books. Many rulers have destroyed texts to erase the memory of enemies or burnt books to stop the spread of 'unacceptable' ideas.

One of the greatest thrills for an archaeologist is to find a text which contains vital historical information. Such a find was the Turin Papyrus, which gave a full list of Egypt's kings. The papyrus was so badly damaged during transport that experts are still trying to piece it back together again.

THE LOSS OF A LONG HISTORY
The Maya and Aztecs covered scrolls of bark or deerskin with pictures of their past. The Spaniards burnt most of them, but had to have a new one, the Codex Mendoza, *made for their king, showing Aztec daily life.*

Have ancient writings influenced our lives? We owe a lot to the wisdom of the past, which has come to us via the Greeks and Romans. The Egyptians invented the 365-day calendar and divided the day into 24 hours. The Babylonians used a system of numbers based on 60, from which we get 360 degrees in a circle, 60 minutes in an hour and 60 seconds in a minute.

MISSING RECORDS

The Library of Alexandria held about 500,000 books, and scholars came from far and wide to read them. Part of it was burnt down during Caesar's campaign in Egypt (48 BC). The rest was destroyed in the AD 270s. Think of all the historical information we have lost!

FATAL OPINIONS

In 221 BC, Zheng, the ruler of Qin province, became the First Emperor of all China. When he heard that some scholars were criticising him, he ordered the burning of all books, old and new, that might be used against him. Later he had 460 scholars executed.

The Dead Sea scrolls

In 1947, a shepherd boy found a cave at Qumran, on the shores of the Dead Sea. It contained some strange, ancient scrolls. Over the next few years, other caves and scrolls were discovered. The study of these texts was held up by scholarly, political and religious rivalry, but they are now becoming available. The scrolls contain biblical texts, writings about the Bible, calendars and hymns. They date from the first centuries BC and AD and were probably hidden during the Jewish revolts of AD 66 and 132, to save them from the Romans. They tell us about religious life before the birth of Christ and so are important to Christians, Jews and Muslims alike.

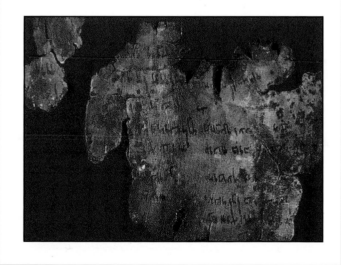

THE SECRET GOSPELS

In the early days of Christianity, there were many different Christian groups. The Gnostics claimed to have secret knowledge, so the Church had their writings destroyed. One Gnostic buried his books at Nag Hammadi in Egypt. They were found by a farmer a few years ago!

WORDS OF WISDOM

A Sibyl was a Roman prophetess (a woman who could foresee the future). One Sibyl sold three books of her writings to King Tarquinius of Rome. The Sibylline prophecies were said to be very accurate and were consulted in times of trouble. They were destroyed by fire in 83 BC, so we will never know how accurate they were.

Why Were They MADE?

People in the past were prepared to go to great lengths to make and build things, using up vast amounts of time and energy (when lives were much shorter than today). What made Stone Age hunters, who needed all their energy to survive, go deep into caves to produce wonders like the Lascaux paintings (see pages 32-33)? It is often difficult to work out how and why things were made. For example, some people still find it hard to believe that so much effort went into building Egypt's pyramids, simply for them to be used as tombs. When we have no texts, just ancient objects or ruins, it is even more difficult to interpret them.

Were ancient towns like modern ones? In the town of Çatal Hüyük (in what is now Turkey), one of the first towns in the world, there were no roads and the houses were entered through a hole in the roof! The town had wide trading links and was very rich. Its citizens may have feared that jealous neighbours might try to attack them.

THE STANDING STONES
The peoples of Bronze Age Europe (3500-1000 BC) have left behind many monuments made of menhirs (upright stones). Some are in long lines; others are in circles. The most famous circle is Stonehenge (left) in southern England. Clearly it was built for religious rites, perhaps related to the Sun, as it faces the midsummer rising and midwinter setting of the Sun. But what of the stones with human faces on the island of Corsica (top)? Do they represent gods, heroes or enemies?

AN EVERLASTING MEMORIAL
Native Americans built the Rock Eagle Effigy Mound in AD 500. Its wingspan is 36 m (120 ft). This is one of the many monuments left by cultures that flourished from 1000 BC to AD 1500 in the Ohio and Mississippi river valleys.

Many built mounds. Some were for burials or had palaces on top. Others must have had religious use, but without written evidence we can only guess at it.

MYSTERIOUS MONUMENTS

Easter Island is only 26 km (15.5 miles) long, yet between AD 600 and 1500, its Polynesian people carved about 1,000 huge stone heads. Were they to honour great ancestors? Civil war and famine meant that statue building ceased.

PICTURES IN THE SAND

The Nazca people flourished along the south coast of Peru from about 200 BC to AD 600. They made lines across the desert by clearing away the stones and exposing the sand. Some of the lines are several kilometres long, some form patterns and others depict huge monkeys, spiders and birds. Were they drawn to please gods in the sky?

Guardians of the dead

Models of servants were placed in the graves of early Chinese kings and nobles, but the First Emperor (221-210 BC) outdid them all! In his tomb at Mount Li, a whole army, sculpted in terracotta, was buried. Over 8,000 life-sized models have been found so far. Most are foot soldiers, but there are also horses, chariots and officers. Three attempts had been made on Zheng's life. He must have wanted a safe afterlife, guarded by his most trusted warriors.

LAWS OF STONE

Emperor Asoka of India (272-231 BC) set up this pillar (right) to mark the spot where the Buddha first taught. Writings on many other pillars across India told of Asoka's laws to encourage peace and happiness in his land.

THE FIRST EGYPTIAN DAM

Recent excavations in Egypt have found that, in about 2600 BC, the Egyptians were building a dam to protect villages from floods rushing down a narrow valley. But a flood destroyed the dam before it was completed.

"*Treasure hunting is as old as Man; scientific archaeology is a modern development, but in its short life... it has done marvels.*"

Sir Leonard Woolley, *Digging up the Past*, 1940

New Ideas and INVESTIGATIONS

Archaeologists are leading the battle to find the lost treasures of the past. Their excavations are still uncovering hidden objects, buildings, texts, cities and even whole civilisations. Historians and language experts then analyse the material. Unlike the archaeologists of the past, today's researchers are able to call upon specialised scientists and the latest modern technology to help them.

Archaeology is now more popular than ever before. Books and TV programmes have made it exciting, and air travel means that thousands of people can now visit the world's wonders. This is great for tourism, but it can also cause archaeological problems. Too many people walking over sites can destroy the very things they have come to see! The caves at Lascaux, France, have been closed since 1963. While they were open to visitors, algae had entered the caves. It spread rapidly and began to destroy the 17,000-year-old paintings (left).

Faces from THE PAST

THE FACE OF PHILIP

In 1977, archaeologists found what they believed was the tomb of the Macedonian king Philip II, but they had no proof. An expert built up a clay face over the skull found in the tomb. It belonged to a man aged 40-50, with a scar over his right eye. We know Philip was wounded (and probably blinded) by an arrow in his eye – so it must be his tomb.

All historians dream about how wonderful it would be to meet people from the past, and, very occasionally, this dream almost comes true. The ancient Egyptians mummified their dead, so we have the thrill of looking at the faces of some of the pharaohs and their subjects. Sometimes, Nature has preserved ancient bodies and faces in an excellent condition. Archaeologists can also turn to the modern police technique of rebuilding a face over the bones of a skull. Experts use clay to build up the muscles, tissues and features such as the nose and mouth, until an ancient face looks out at them once again.

The 'Ice Man'

One autumn day, about 5,000 years ago, a man was trudging through the Alps when he was caught in a blizzard. He lay down to sleep, and never awoke. His body, preserved by the ice, was found in 1991. We are getting valuable information about life in his time from his possessions. But why was he all alone? Was he a trader, a shepherd or a priest? Had he left his village in a hurry?

BURIED IN THE BOG

The bogs of northern Europe have preserved many bodies, slain then thrown into the mud. We know that Iron Age people often made human sacrifices to their gods and goddesses. Were these bodies sacrificial victims? Some may have been criminals being punished or volunteers who hoped to bring luck to their tribe by pleasing the gods.

A GRAND SEND-OFF

Because their graves were cut into ground that was permanently frozen, the burials of nomadic chieftains and their families have been well preserved in the Altai Mountains of Kazakhstan. Objects of wood, cloth and leather, sacrificed horses and tattooed bodies have all survived since 400-200 BC.

VICTIMS OF VESUVIUS

In AD 79, Mount Vesuvius in Italy erupted and the city of Pompeii was buried by ash and pumice stone. Most of its inhabitants fled, but those who stayed (about 2,000) were suffocated by fumes. Their bodies decayed, but the ash hardened round them, preserving their impressions. By filling the hollows with plaster, archaeologists can make replicas of the ancient bodies.

A GAZE FROM THE PAST

She lived in ancient Egypt and was about 14 when she died. Her mummy was reduced to bones. She suffered from a nose complaint and had lost both legs from the knee down, but we do not know if this happened before or after her death. This mysterious girl's face has been rebuilt on her skull and even given make-up.

THE FACE OF A KING

Timur Leng (Timur the Lame, 1336-1405), known in the West as Tamerlaine, carved an empire in the Middle East and Central Asia. When historians opened his tomb, they asked experts to build up a face over the skull they found. It clearly showed the strong character of the ruthless war-lord (above)!

What can modern medicine tell us about people of the past?
Medical knowledge can help historians. Most statues of Alexander the Great show him with his chin in the air and his head to one side. People thought it showed his arrogance. Recently, two doctors have suggested that he may have had a rare eye disease called Brown's Syndrome. The only way for sufferers to see properly is to hold their head in the way shown by the statues.

Methods of the FUTURE

Science, technology, medicine – all have made rapid progress over the last few years, greatly helping scholars and archaeologists. There are new techniques to help them find things and others to help them date those that they find. They can reconstruct an ancient landscape by examining and analysing pollen and tiny organisms from a site. Medical techniques can now reveal more about ancient bodies and analyse blood and DNA. Science can help to conserve things better than ever and to detect fakes, too – forgers, beware!

Do people ever fake ancient finds?
The skull of 'Piltdown Man', found in 1912, was hailed as a 'missing link' in evolution. But in 1953, it was proved to be a fake. An old trunk has been found that belonged to a curator at the Natural History Museum, London, at the time. It is stained with the same chemicals as those used by the hoaxer!

THE PRIDE OF THE FLEET
The Mary Rose *sank near Plymouth, England, in 1545. It settled on its side on the sea bed, where silt preserved one half. Raised in 1982, it is providing many details about Tudor life and ship-building.*

WHAT LIES BELOW?
If the ground is suitable, time and money can be saved by using special equipment to find underground hollows, indicating tombs. If a tomb is found, a hole is drilled and a camera is put in. Photos are taken to see if it is worth opening.

VIRTUAL HISTORY
Have you ever looked at ruins and wondered what the original *building was like? Thanks to computers, you can now find out. Plans of a ruin can be used to produce a 3-D reconstruction. You can see the building as its original occupants knew it.*

AERIAL ARCHAEOLOGY

A ruined building or a large mound, whether it is a tomb or the remains of a long-lost city, is easy to find. But a site that has been flattened and ploughed over for centuries is very hard to spot. The soil over ancient walls is not as deep, so plants do not grow as well there. This causes patterns in the crops. You cannot see these on the ground, but they show up in photos taken from the air.

RESTORING ITS GLORY

Egypt's Queen Nefertari owes a double debt to modern technology! Engineers lifted her temple at Abu Simbel above the waters of Lake Nasser. Now scientists have preserved the exquisite paintings in her tomb, which were being destroyed by salt crystals that had formed under the paint and were pushing it off the walls.

HAPPY FAMILIES

DNA is a substance in our body, inherited from both our parents. It determines how we look. Everyone's DNA is unique. Police scientists analyse DNA to identify criminals. Such analysis can tell archaeologists if bodies are related. It is now being used on Egyptian mummies.

Underwater magic

The Second World War (1939-45), saw the development of the Aqua-Lung, which allows divers to swim and use their arms freely. This led to the birth of marine archaeology. Dozens of shipwrecks have yielded up details of their cargoes and the secrets of their construction. Buildings drowned by the sea may also be excavated. Blocks from the lighthouse at Alexandria have been found recently, with statues that once adorned the city.

What next?

We have yet to identify Helen of Troy. Robin Hood remains hidden in the forest and Solomon's mines are a tempting prize. There are lost people, treasures, cities and civilisations to be found, and new tools with which to find them. For archaeologists, the past has an exciting future. You can enjoy it, too.

TIME

c. 15,000 BC Lascaux
cave paintings are made

c. 3100-30 BC Egypt flourishes
c. 3000-1450 BC Minoan civilisation

c. 2950-1500 BC Stonehenge built in 3 stages
c. 2600 BC First Egyptian dam started
c. 2500-1700 BC Civilisation in Indus Valley
c. 2500-1500 BC Bactrian culture at its peak
c. 2000 BC Hittites arrive in Anatolia (Turkey)

c. 1900-1000 Mycenaean civilisation flourishes
c. 1450 BC Thera volcano destroys Minoans
c. 1367-1350 BC Akhenaten rules Egypt
c. 1190 BC 'Sea Peoples' defeat Hittites
c. 1000 BC-AD 1500 Native American cultures
flourish in Ohio & Mississippi river valleys

c. 800 BC-100 BC Greek civilisation
c. 753 BC-AD 476 Roman civilisation
c. 612 BC City of Babylon rebuilt
c. 550 BC-AD 350 Meroe at its peak
c. 432 BC Statue of Zeus built at Olympia
400s BC-AD 200s Petra is an important city
c. 280 BC Lighthouse at Alexandria built
c. 272-231 BC Emperor Asoka rules India
c. 221-210 BC Zheng rules China
c. 200 BC-AD 600 Nazca lines are created
c. 83 BC Sibylline prophecies are destroyed
51-30 BC Cleopatra VII rules Egypt

AD 60-62 Queen Boudicca leads
British revolt against Romans
AD 66/132 Jewish revolts
against rule of the Romans
AD 79 Town of Pompeii
destroyed by eruption
of Mount Vesuvius

LINE

AD **270s** *Remains of Library*
of Alexandria are destroyed
AD **462** *Statue of Zeus destroyed*
AD **476** *Roman Empire collapses*
c. AD **500** *Rock Eagle Mound, USA;*
King Arthur thought to exist, England
c. AD **600-1500** *Easter Island statues erected*
AD **800s** *Khmers build Angkor Wat & Thom*

1336-1405 *Timur Leng (Tamerlaine) lives*
1375 *Lighthouse at Alexandria is destroyed*
1521-22 *Tenochtitlan destroyed by the Spaniards*
1545 *Mary Rose sinks off the English coast*
1748-present *Excavations at Pompeii &*
neighbouring town of Herculaneum, Italy
1843 *John Stephens finds Chichén Itzá*
1870 *Heinrich Schliemann finds Troy*
1876 *Schliemann excavates Mycenae*
1893 *Arthur Evans finds Minoan remains*
1911 *Hiram Bingham finds Machu Picchu*
1912 *'Piltdown Man' bones discovered*
(but are proved to be a hoax in 1953)
1922 *Howard Carter opens tomb of King*
Tutankhamun; Leonard Woolley excavates Ur
1940 *Schoolboys find Lascaux cave paintings*
1945-48 *Mortimer Wheeler excavates Indus Valley*
1947 *Dead Sea scrolls found in cave at Qumran*
1974 *Tomb of First Emperor of China discovered*
1977 *Tomb of Philip II of Macedonia discovered*
1980s *Examination of Chinese noblewoman*
1991 *Frozen man discovered, wonderfully*
preserved in glacier in Austrian mountains
1992 *Minoan paintings discovered*
in ancient Egyptian tombs
1995 *Tomb containing over 50*
sons of King Ramesses II
discovered in Egypt
1996 *Tomb of Queen*
Nefertari reopened

INDEX

Picture Credits (*t-top, m-middle, b-bottom, r-right, l-left*): 4-5, 11 – Ancient Art & Architecture Collection; 13 – Bruce Coleman Collection; 17, 24, 29, 33, 34, 37 – Frank Spooner Pictures; 18 – York Archaeological Trust; 23 – Mary Evans Picture Library; 31 – James Davis Travel Photography.